ITALY

Balanced on the Edge of Time

by Anthony DiFranco

Dillon Press, Inc.   Minneapolis, Minnesota 55415

Acknowledgments

For help and support in preparing this book, the author wishes to acknowledge his wife Adrienne, JoAnn Devenuti, Lawrence Epstein, Nicholas Marino, and Esther Newberg. Thanks are also due to Arba Sicula, Inc., a Brooklyn-based, nonprofit national Sicilian-American cultural organization, for sharing information on Sicilian proverbs and nicknames. For supplying photographs for the text, the author wishes to acknowledge especially the assistance of Mr. Giorgio Columbo of the Italian Cultural Institute, as well as the Italian Government Travel Office and Alitalia Airlines.

Library of Congress Cataloging in Publication Data

DiFranco, Anthony Mario.
  Italy, balanced on the edge of time.

  (Discovering our heritage)
  Bibliography: p. 124
  Includes index.
  Summary: Presents Italian history, traditions, social life and customs, education, and sports, with a chapter on Italians in the United States. Includes a list of Italian consulates in the United States and Canada, and a glossary.
  1. Italy—Social life and customs—Juvenile literature. 2. Italian Americans—Juvenile literature.[1. Italy] I. Title. II. Series.
  DG441.D53   1982   945   82-17722
  ISBN 0-87518-229-1

Dillon Press, Inc., 500 South Third Street
Minneapolis, Minnesota 55415

Printed in the United States of America

Contents

Fast Facts About Italy

Official Name: *Repubblica Italiana* (Italian Republic)

Capital: Rome

Location: Southern Europe; Italy is a peninsula that extends southward into the Mediterranean Sea. The country also includes two large islands, Sicily and Sardinia.

Area: 116,314 square miles (301,252 square kilometers); the greatest distances in Italy are 708 miles (1,139 kilometers) from north to south and 130 miles (209 kilometers) from east to west. Italy has 2,685 miles (4,321 kilometers) of coastline.

Elevation: *Highest*—a point on Monte Albino (Mont Blanc) 15,521 feet (4,731 meters) above sea level. *Lowest*—sea level along the coast.

Population: *Estimated 1982 Population*—58,159,000; *Distribution*—60 percent of the people live in or near cities; 40 percent live in rural areas; *Density*—500 persons per square mile (193 persons per square kilometer).

Form of Government: Republic; *Head of Government*—premier.

Important Products: Fruits, grains, livestock, olives, potatoes, sugar beets; automobiles, chemicals, clothing, leather products, machine tools, petroleum products, ships, steel, textiles, typewriters, wine.

Basic Unit of Money: Lira.

Major Languages: Italian (and regional dialects).

Major Religion: 98 percent of Italians are Roman Catholic.

Flag: Three broad, vertical stripes of green, white and orange.

National Anthem: "*Inno di Mameli*" ("Hymn of Mameli")

Major Holidays: Carnevale season—January 17 through the beginning of Lent; Easter Day; Ascension Day—forty days after Easter; Day of the Dead—November 2; Christmas Day— December 25.

1. A Land of Old and New

Imagine a land where time seems mixed up. In one town, men in old-time costumes race on horseback. In another, fast cars speed around a track. Out in the country, children drive oxen in the fields, while in the city they shop in new malls. Think of movie theaters and old temples, shacks and skyscrapers. The land you are imagining is Italy.

Italy lies across the Atlantic Ocean. It juts down from Europe into a large sea called the Mediterranean. Long and mountainous, it stretches through the sea almost to Africa.

You can easily pick out Italy's shape on a map because it looks like a high-heeled boot. The toe of the boot points to the island of Sicily, and the knee points to another large island, Sardinia. Both are part of Italy, along with about seventy smaller islands.

Italy is not nearly as large as America. In fact, it's barely roomier than Arizona, the sixth largest U.S. state. Yet it has more than 58 million people, which means that in most places Italy is more crowded than the United States.

Still, it is one of the larger countries of Europe. Though not very wide, Italy spans 708 miles (1,139 kilometers) from north to south. Because it's so long, the weather and scenery change from one region to another. In addition, Italy's many mountains make natural barriers that divide the country into several parts.

On the world globe, Italy lies at the same latitude, or distance from the equator, as the northern half of the United States. Its climate, though, is milder because the seas help to keep the weather warmer during the winter.

In the north, tall mountains called the Alps keep out cold winds. The plain at their foot has damp, warm summers and cold winters with rain and snow. A city in this plain, Milan, has more rain and fog than foggy London.

In the middle of the boot, winters are mild. Summers are hot, but not terribly so. The air is dry, and the sky is a lovely blue. Artists love to catch the light and color in this part of "sunny Italy."

In the south, summers are very hot. Palm trees grow, and the people harvest oranges, lemons, and limes. Winters are rainy but mild. If you lived in Naples, which lies at the same latitude as New York City, your house would need almost no heat.

Sicily in the south is only a short distance from Africa. Sometimes the *sirocco*, a hot wind from the Sahara Desert, blows across the Mediterranean Sea

A family picks apples in an orchard in northern Italy.

to Italy. Often it carries red desert dust. Then, if rain falls, the rain is red. Italians say the sirocco puts them in a sour mood.

The people in Italy's different regions have lived in their land a very long time. At first they were many separate tribes. Over time, these tribes mixed together, and others from beyond the Alps joined them. Today's Italians are a blend of all these groups. Most are dark, sturdy, slender, and rather short. Their skin has a faint olive tint, and their hair is so fine that wig makers come from all over the world to buy it. Not all Italians fit this description, though. In fact, some are tall, pale, and blond.

Whatever their looks, Italians share much in common. They receive the same basic schooling, and nearly everyone speaks the Italian language. Almost all of the people belong to the Roman Catholic church.

The pope, head of the Catholic church, lives in the Vatican. This is a tiny country inside the city of Rome. Imagine a country so small that you can walk through it in minutes! Yet it has its own railway and post office, and it holds the world's biggest church, Saint Peter's. On some days huge crowds come to see the pope. "*Il Papa!*" they cheer when he appears at his window.

San Marino, the other small country within Italy, sits atop a mountain in the upper part of the boot. It

Hundreds of thousands of people gather in front of Saint Peter's church in the Vatican to hear Pope John Paul II deliver his Easter message to the world.

claims to be the oldest republic in the world.

For a long time, there were a number of independent areas within what is now Italy. Until 1860, the country was made up of separate regions. Each had its own customs and language. People from Tuscany thought of themselves as Tuscans, not Italians. Those from Sicily were Sicilians. Even today, many Italians think of themselves as coming from a particular region or city, and many speak a regional dialect, or variety of language. To understand why, let's take a closer look at the mountains that divide Italy into small parts.

The mountains start in the north where Italy joins its European neighbors. There the Alps are shared with France, Switzerland, and Austria. *Monte Bianco*, "White Mountain," is the tallest, almost three miles (five kilometers) high. Nearby is the Matterhorn, which is called "Stag Mountain" by the Italians because its shape reminds them of a wild deer. Between these two mountains is the Great Saint Bernard Pass. Here, for hundreds of years, monks used Saint Bernard dogs to help save people lost in storms.

Farther to the east are the Dolomites. These mountains have smaller, steeper cliffs, perfect for climbing. In summer the hills ring with the music of cowbells.

In the past, traveling across the mountains into Italy was a difficult journey. And yet armies have often crossed them. In 218 B.C., a general named Hannibal brought thirty-seven war elephants over the Alps along with his soldiers. The Italians of the time fought for years to defeat this invader.

Today, tunnels make the crossing easy. There is a famous one under Monte Bianco, which is seven miles long and took six years to build. The Italians began digging on one side of the mountain. The

Cortina d'Ampezzo is a lovely winter resort area in the Dolomites.

French dug on the other side. When they met in the middle, the tunnel was only nine inches out of line!

At the foot of the Italian Alps is a chain of lovely lakes. Wheat, corn, flax, and vegetables are grown in the fertile plain below, the Po Valley. Large, busy cities rise there, too. City families visit the lakes to cool off during the warm summer months.

City children also enjoy trips to the Italian Riviera on the northwest coast. This fine seashore has white, sandy beaches, hotels, and shops. It is busiest during *Ferragosto*, the last two weeks in August, when most Italians leave the hot cities. Stores close, streets empty, and the beaches are crowded.

Starting near the Riviera in the north, more mountains run down the boot to Sicily. They're called the Apennines, the backbone of Italy. Once oak, birch, and pine forests covered them, but the trees were cut down long ago.

Now these low mountains yield a hard living, especially in the east where most roads are too steep for cars. Farmers grow what they can in the rainy season. In the dry season, they search for grass for their goats. Nothing is wasted. Even the steep slopes are planted with grape vines.

In the west, the land is better. Farms here are said to be the best tended in the world. Grains, fruits, olives, cattle, and pigs are raised.

Farmers harvest hay on a hillside in the fertile Po Valley.

Some of the mountains in the south are known for blowing their top. Mount Etna in Sicily is an active volcano. Near the city of Naples is a volcano named Vesuvius. Every so often it erupts, spilling hot lava on the towns below. Though the last big blast was in 1944, the cone still rumbles and smokes. It's not surprising that both *lava* and *volcano* are Italian words.

At the foot of Vesuvius lies the ancient Roman city of Pompeii. Almost two thousand years ago, in A.D. 79, Pompeii was buried by ash in a great, sudden eruption. Two hundred years ago, scientists began to dig out the remains of the city. They found houses, shops, and bakeries with bread still in the ovens! Sadly, many of the city's people had been trapped by the hot lava. It made perfect molds of their dead bodies.

Italy has earthquakes, too. A bad one struck near Naples on November 23, 1981. More than one hundred towns were destroyed, nearly three thousand people died, and hundreds of thousands more lost their homes.

In spite of the volcanic eruptions and earth-quakes, Italians enjoy living in the mountains. A hillside village is a happy place to grow up because children spend most of their time with their families. They help in the vineyards and care for pigs or goats.

If they wish, they can be alone with their thoughts.

Unlike country life, city life is crowded and noisy. Still, the best way to know Italy is to know its cities. Most are very beautiful. Rome, the capital, is the largest. It's in the middle of the boot beside the Tiber River. Because this very old city was built on seven hills, children here are used to climbing steps.

Rome's streets are filled with people in colorful clothes. Soldiers and sailors wear bright caps, and in summer policemen dress all in white. Nuns and priests are everywhere. Certain students wear gowns of purple, blue, or deep red. Those in red are nick-named "boiled lobsters."

The children of Rome can watch puppet shows in the parks. When they get hungry, they can buy drinks and hot foods from vendors. *Gelato*, or ice cream, is sold from specially made motorcycle carts. Italians really like ice cream. In fact, they invented it.

To the south of Rome are charming cities such as Palermo in Sicily. Palermo overlooks a curved bay called the Golden Shell because of its orange trees. Naples, too, overlooks a lovely horseshoe bay. "See Naples and die," is an old saying. It means you may never hope to see a prettier place in your life.

Most of Italy's large cities lie to the north of Rome. Pisa is the home of the famous leaning tower, which is part of a beautiful church. When workmen were building the bell tower long ago, it began to sink. They waited many years, and then built the top part as straight as they could. The tower leaned even more, and today it is still slowly sinking.

On the northeast coast is a very old and beautiful city which is unlike any other in Italy. Venice has water in place of streets. Special boats called *gondolas* transport people from place to place. Gondolas are pushed along by boatmen with poles. At night a lantern on the gondola lights the way under the bridges. Venice also has motorboats, ferryboats, garbage boats, ambulance boats, funeral boats—boats for everything.

Gondolas travel along the famous Grand Canal in Venice.

*Venice has boats for everything—including this floating
vegetable market.*

To the west of Venice lie the cities of industry. Genoa, Milan, and Turin form the "iron triangle." In these bustling cities, workers make everything from shoes to airplanes. Genoa is also a big port where thousands of ships dock each year.

Milan has subways, tall buildings, and fancy stores and restaurants. It is sometimes called the "New York of Europe." Alfa Romeo cars are made in this city, and the famous Monza autodrome is nearby.

The real city of cars, though, is Turin, where Fiat and Lancia cars are made. At the yearly auto fair, Ferraris, Maserattis, and other fine cars are on display.

Many Italians like speed and racing. In fact, some of them drive as if they were in a race. Luckily, Italy has an excellent highway system. Its high-speed roads gave the idea of expressways to the rest of the world.

Italian cities, though, were not meant for cars. Traffic jams in the narrow streets are so bad that drivers go onto the sidewalk to get by. Their cars are tiny, because fuel is costly. Even so, drivers don't have enough room to park. In Palermo special trucks with cranes hoist cars from no-parking zones. But other drivers follow the trucks around so that they can park in the spaces cleared by the cranes!

Problems like this one came with *Il Boom*. That is what Italians call their fast growth since 1945. For the

Auto workers on the assembly line of the Alfa Romeo plant in Milan.

next twenty-five years, their country grew faster than
it ever had before.

Despite the changes, Italians value their old ways.
They still have joyous festivals for their patron saints,
and they still treasure their art and history, even in the
iron triangle. The people of Milan are proud of their
glass-roofed mall with its fine shops. But they are also
proud of the six-hundred-year-old church that stands
beside it.

Italy today, then, is a rich blend of old and new.
Its people are pleased with the new ways they have
brought to their old land.

2. *Operas, Comic Books, and Holy Days*

On a street in Italy there are faces of every kind. Some are dark, with deep, shining eyes, while others are blond and blue-eyed, with sharp features. Some are bushy-haired and hook-nosed. Still others have the "Greek" noses that seem to grow in a straight line from their foreheads. All are Italians.

Since earliest times, invaders of many races have come to Italy. Slaves from Greece, Egypt, Spain, and elsewhere were also brought to the country. That is why no single type of Italian exists today. And after so much mixing, the people from each part of the land have rather different ways.

In the northern cities, there are many office and factory workers. Cars fill the streets, and well-dressed crowds hurry along the sidewalks. Many northerners take pride in being good at business. Those from Genoa claim to be the smartest. "Not even the devil can outwit a Genoese," they boast.

Tuscany is the land of blue skies and dark, pointed cypress trees. Here some people keep neat farms, while others are clever craftspeople and artists. In the city of Florence, children learn weaving, leather working, and jewelry making from their parents.

Highways in busy Genoa soar high above the city. Italians have been known for their roadbuilding skills since the times of the Romans.

Rome, to the south of Tuscany, is a busy and noisy city. Its people act as if they know they are at the center of everything. "All roads lead to Rome," one of their sayings goes. Dwellers in such a big, old city tend to be down-to-earth. They believe that they have seen just about everything there is to see.

In crowded Naples, voices are louder and hands wave freely. The smell of onions and hot cheese drifts

These Sicilians, dressed in traditional costumes, can see for miles from the hillside overlooking their town.

from the many pizza shops. Even in the poor neighborhoods, the people seem friendly and quick to laugh. Perhaps our image of Italians as cheerful street vendors or waiters is taken from these spirited Neapolitans.

That happy image, though, would not be right for most Sicilians. They like to have fun, too, but in public they tend to be serious and proud. After ages of harsh rule by outsiders, Sicilians are watchful over their families and their honor. Girls and women have just begun to take part in life outside the home. Even though Sicilians are suspicious of strangers, they can be the warmest of friends to those they trust.

In addition to being a land of parts, Italy is a land of "tongues." Most Italians use at least two languages. One is the language of the local region. The problem is that the local languages, called dialects, are not much alike. Using them, a boy from Lombardy can't talk to one from Naples. A girl from Sicily can't understand one from Rome.

To talk to one another, they must use the second, or standard, Italian language. Its use became widespread about six hundred years ago. A man named Dante Alighieri wrote a long, beautiful poem in the Tuscan dialect, *The Divine Comedy*. Italians liked it so much that the Tuscan dialect became widely used throughout the land.

This national language has such a lovely sound that Italians enjoy using it well. They admire a quick mind and a tongue that can draw hidden meanings from words. It's not surprising that they have learned to use their hands and faces in speech, too. In fact, these gestures are an important part of what Italians say.

Some Italian gestures are easy to understand. Thumping the fingers against the forehead is a way of telling someone, "Your head is full of stones!" But what does it mean when a man simply shuts his eyes without moving his face? "I will do what must be done," he is saying. A lifted eyebrow, a stiffened chin—there are hundreds of signs like these. They are used so much that they are almost a language in themselves. To Italians, talking is an art.

Italians are also clever at giving nicknames. In Sicily and elsewhere, these joke names sometimes become people's real names. For example, a Sicilian with the name Ciciri would be called "Chickpea" in English. He or one of his ancestors was a big eater of chickpeas. Scannaporci, "Pig-killer," is a name for someone whose ancestors slaughtered pigs, and Burrittuni, "Big-cap" is for someone who likes fancy hats. No explaining is needed for Aricchiazza, "Big-ears." But what about Funciaredda, "Little-mouth"? This is a joke name for a thick-lipped person!

We have already looked at some of the ways in which Italians differ. But what about the ways in which they are alike? There are many, for truly Italians are one people.

For one thing, they share a love of family. Everywhere in Italy families do things together. In the countryside, children work alongside their parents. In the cities, they shop, go to church, eat, relax, and watch TV together.

A woman and child make toys near the northern city of Bolzano.

In most families the father is the head. Everyone in the household shows him respect. While the father is the head, the mother is the family's heart. She is free with her love to her children. Even when they're grown, they feel a special closeness to her. *Mamma mia!* "My mother!" is a saying heard often in Italy. In many families mothers and sons have a special closeness. Married sons still spend much time with their mothers, and a visit to *nonna*, grandmother, is a common treat for grandchildren.

Today in the industrial cities, family life is changing. Often both wives and husbands go to work. A new law has made them equals in marriage, and another law has made divorce legal, though hard to get. Women's rights groups have made gains, too. There are even outlaw bands just for women. In one city, such a gang bombed a dress shop because it thought the fashions were insulting to women.

Still, the old family ways are the most common, especially in the south. Many Italians like large families. They think that having healthy and happy children is the greatest blessing in life. A handsome child is fussed over even by strangers. Parents spend much time holding, kissing, and playing with their children. Older sisters and brothers, aunts, uncles, and grandparents help care for them, too.

Children must learn the ways of the family while

they are very young. They must obey and respect their elders. As they grow, they must help care for the house and the younger children. Young people learn that life is serious but not sad. A lovely morning, a tasty meal, a friendly chat—these simple things make life sweet for Italian families.

Both boys and girls learn to groom themselves and to dress neatly. Children wear handsome, but not showy, clothes. They like white shirts and blouses, pretty sweaters, white stockings, and shined shoes. Smocks are worn to help keep clothes clean. Even the poorest parents will find a way to dress their children well.

Parents and children may be only part of an Italian family. Often grandparents live in the household, too, and join in all the family does. They care for the children when mothers must work, and they teach them practical lessons about life. *Pazienza,* "patience," is a lesson they repeat many times. Since grandparents and children have a lot of time for each other, they are often very close.

Aunts, uncles, and cousins may also be part of an Italian family. In the country married sons bring their wives to live in their parents' home. Then the grandmother can watch the small children while their mother and father do the farm work. At mealtime a crowd of people sits down to eat. The main meal, eaten at about two in the afternoon, is a time for fun and sharing. The grown-ups talk and laugh around the big table. They listen to what the young ones have to say, too.

In the cities family life is different. Still, entire families get together for big meals. Italians enjoy eating, and anything they do is more fun with food.

Italians like eating outdoors best of all. If the day is cool, they set up their tables in the sunshine. If it's warm, they eat on shady terraces or beneath roofs of vines. As they eat, they talk, laugh, and argue. They raise their voices and bang the table to make a point. They aren't mad; in fact, they're having a good time. After all, eating, talking, and being outside are three things that nearly all Italians like.

While Italians enjoy eating and talking, they are good workers, too. They are best at jobs that call for special skills. Italians make fine furniture, lace, clothing, pottery, glassware, and jewelry. They like to do a job from start to finish.

Many people, however, must work at dull factory jobs. To make their work more pleasant, they often sing while working. Most Italians share a love of music, especially the fancy musical plays called operas. The favorites were written about a century ago by famous Italian composers—Verdi, Puccini, and Rossini. Today homemakers still hum these

An inside view of the Teatro dell'Opera, Rome's opera house.

songs as they hang out the laundry. Workers sing them on their jobs.

There are opera houses in all parts of Italy. A world famous one is La Scala in Milan. At the San Carlo Opera House in Naples, Italians cheer madly when they hear a beautiful voice. They boo when the singing isn't good enough.

Other kinds of music are popular, too. Young people listen to jazz and rock on radios and juke-boxes. In the country, the people play bagpipes, fid-dles, guitars, and mandolins. Southerners may gather around the music to do a lively dance called the *tarantella*. It is named for the city of Taranto, which also gave its name to the hairy tarantula spider.

Italians enjoy art as much as music. Their cities are filled with churches, statues, and fountains. Michelangelo and Leonardo da Vinci, Italian artists of the past, are ranked among the world's greatest painters and sculptors. For centuries painters have come here from all over the world to study.

Italians have mastered new arts such as movie-making, too. In the late 1940s, they won world praise for a new style of film, called neo-realism. It showed life in a more real way than Hollywood's make-believe movies did at that time. Some award-winning films in this new style were *Open City, Shoeshine,* and *Bicycle Thief.*

Children in Italy like American-style western movies, cartoons, and comic books. One favorite hero of the comics is the Red Devil. Another is a little mouse called Topolino. Most Italian homes have TV sets now, and children enjoy watching their favorite shows in the late afternoon.

Both young and old Italians like to meet friends

and talk. One place to do this is a café. Here people stand at a counter and enjoy coffee or wine while they chat with friends. They may sit at a table and do business, too. Some cafés provide free paper, pencils, and newspapers. In the big Italian cities, people often go to the *galleria* to meet friends. Inside this glass-roofed mall are busy cafés, stores, and movie houses.

Many Italians are eager to ask questions and to talk about their lives, even to strangers. Among friends they are even more at home. Men walk arm in arm in the street, and women kiss when greeting. This warmth is what makes holy days a joyous time for all Italians.

Once a year each town gives its patron saint a festival that includes singing, dancing, fireworks, and, of course, food. The people dress the saint's statue in rich clothes and carry it through the streets. The merrymaking goes on until late at night.

All year round, the people feel close to their saints. In return for prayers and gifts, they hope to be protected from harm. Not every Italian is religious, but religion seems to touch most parts of life. People wear religious crosses and charms. Churches are richly decorated, and priests are given great respect. Christmas, Easter, and other holy days are the most important celebrations of the year. For children birthdays take second place to "name days." On these days children honor the saints after whom they were named.

Operas, comic books, and holy days—all are part of Italian ways. To understand how these ways came to be, we must go back in time to the Italy of long ago. For in Italy's rich past are the seeds of the land and people of today.

3. The Parade of the Past

Italy is both a very old and a very young country. It was the center of a vast empire long before Columbus came to America. After many years that empire fell apart, and from its pieces grew most of the modern nations of Europe. But Italy, where everything had begun, was one of the last to become a modern nation.

Italians cannot easily forget their long past. Ancient houses and temples still stand in many places. When workers dig roads and subways, they keep finding buried things from long ago. Then the digging must stop until scientists come and have a look. Some people complain that the country's growth is cluttered by its past.

Others, though, find the past rich and exciting. Once workers dug up a carved coffin. Inside was the body of a young girl which had been wrapped in special cloths to keep it lifelike. Though the girl had died fifteen hundred years before, her face was still soft and lovely. Words on the coffin told that her name was Julia, the daughter of a rich Roman. Crowds came to marvel over this reminder of their country's past.

Still used for performances, this ancient Roman theater in Trieste is surrounded by modern buildings.

Italy's story begins with the ancient city of Rome. According to myth, this city was built by Romulus and Remus, the twin sons of the war god, Mars. After their birth, their evil uncle tried to drown them in the river Tiber. But the river stopped its course! Then a she-wolf came and adopted the boys. When they were grown, Romulus built a city on seven hills. It was named "Rome" after him.

Rome filled with men from other places. The men had no wives because nearby tribes would not allow their young women near the new city. Finally the Roman men stole these women for their wives. A war broke out, but the new wives rushed between the fighting men. They forced their fathers and brothers to make peace with their new husbands.

Over time the Romans became the rulers of all Italy. They farmed the land and kept their weapons ready to defend it. Though fierce in war, they honored their families and their gods.

The Romans admired courage in both men and women. One legend tells about Lucretia, a Roman woman who was famous for her beauty and goodness. Her husband unwisely boasted of her to Sextus, son of Tarquin the Proud, the seventh king of Rome. This evil man attacked Lucretia when her husband was away.

The next day, Lucretia told her husband how she

had been shamed by the son of Tarquin. Then she killed herself with a dagger she had hidden in her clothes. The Roman people were very angry when they saw her body. They rose up and cast out Tarquin and his sons.

Porsenna, another king, decided to help Tarquin regain his throne. He led his army against Rome and camped for the night outside the city. The Romans were in great danger.

A brave Roman named Mutius crept into the enemy camp and made his way through all the soldiers to Porsenna's tent. Inside he found two men. Mutius rushed up and stabbed to death the one he thought was Porsenna. Then he fled.

Porsenna, however, was the other man. Mutius was caught and brought back before him. To Porsenna's questions, he would only answer that he was a Roman. To show what he meant, he laid his right hand in an altar of burning coals. He showed no sign of pain. Three hundred other young Romans, Mutius said, had also sworn to sneak into the camp to kill Porsenna.

Porsenna was stunned at the courage of the Romans. He decided to make peace with them and quickly led his army away. Mutius, afterward known as Scaevola ("Lefty"), had saved the city!

Hateful of the memory of kings, the Romans

established a republic in which they elected their leaders. They defended their republic with well-trained *legions* of soldiers. The Roman legions crossed the Alps and took control of one place after the next. Finally, much of Europe, Asia Minor, and North Africa were under the rule of Rome.

One famous commander of the legions was Julius Caesar. He won many wars and then became the ruler of Rome. Afterward he made himself emperor for life. Other Roman leaders, remembering the evils of the old kings, decided to kill him. Brutus, one of the leaders, was Caesar's friend. He agreed to help only because he loved the republic more than he loved his friend.

Caesar did not try to defend himself when he saw Brutus among the killers. He covered his face and fell dead from the stab wounds. In the civil war that followed, Brutus was also killed. The republic ended for good, and the empire took its place.

Jesus was born during the first emperor's rule. He was put to death in the part of the empire known as Judaea.

Later his followers, the Christians, became a problem to the Roman rulers. They spread their belief in a God who was above the emperors. Because the Christians were treated as enemies, often they had to worship in secret. At times they were arrested and killed.

In the Colosseum, a stadium in Rome, they were given to wild, hungry animals. Crowds also watched slaves fight to the death there.

More and more, cruelty took the place of the old Roman courage. The whole empire grew weak. Three hundred years after Christ's time, it split in two. The eastern half stayed strong for another thousand years, but Italy, in the western half, was invaded by warlike tribes. In A.D. 476, Rome fell.

This first part of Italy's past lasted for twelve hundred years. Since the sad end of Rome's power, fifteen hundred more years have passed. During this long time, the people of Italy have seen more hardship than glory.

After Rome fell, a "dark age" began in Italy. Since there was no longer a central government, the popes, the leaders of the Christian church, helped rule the land. They taught Christianity to the invading tribes. At last, in A.D. 800, Pope Leo III crowned Charlemagne emperor of the Romans. Charlemagne, king of a strong tribe called the Franks, had helped the popes defeat invaders. He and the leaders who followed him ruled what became known as the Holy Roman Empire.

This empire, however, was not strong enough to hold together for long. Over hundreds of years, the area that is now Italy broke apart into three different regions. In the north, such cities as Venice, Genoa, Florence, Milan, and Pisa grew rich. They became city-states, which were independent areas with their own laws and armies. In the central part, the popes ruled. In the south, foreign kings took control.

The slow mending of these splits began in the north. The city-states began to trade with the cities of northern Europe. They also "discovered" the Orient.

In 1295 a man named Marco Polo came back to Venice after a twenty-five-year journey to faraway lands. None of his friends knew him, for he had gone away with his father when he was only seventeen. To prove who he was, he gave a banquet. At the meal he wore strange and beautiful clothes. These, he said, came from the far-off land of Cathay, or China, where he had been all those years. He told his friends how vast and rich Cathay was. As proof, he dumped piles of diamonds, rubies, and other gems on the table. At last the guests believed his story. They greeted their long-lost friend Marco Polo.

Trading with foreign lands helped bring about a big change in Italy. In Italian cities a new interest in art and science began that spread throughout Europe. Italian writers and artists tried out exciting new ideas during this time, which is known as the Renaissance. Money for these works of art came from the popes and the rich ruling families of the cities.

Two of Italy's and the world's greatest artists lived during the Renaissance. Michelangelo made his wonderful statues, and Leonardo da Vinci painted the *Mona Lisa* and *The Last Supper*. Leonardo also tried for years to design an airplane that would fly.

Galileo, a great scientist of the time, watched the heavens with his new telescopes. His bold experiments showed that the earth moved around the sun. But the old beliefs, which were supported by the Catholic church, had made the earth the center of the

Michelangelo made this statue at the Basilica di San Pietro in Vincoli.

universe. Church leaders brought Galileo to trial. Since the punishment for false teaching could be death, Galileo took back what he had said. Yet he was right, and the knowledge that he had gained was an important first step in modern science.

Even during the Renaissance, Italy was a divided land. The city-states fought so much among themselves that foreign powers moved in. For more than three hundred years, much of Italy was ruled by Spanish, French, and Austrian kings.

In the rest of Europe, machines and factories were appearing. People were electing their rulers, and such modern nations as France and the United States were forming. Italy, though, remained divided and ruled by foreigners.

At last, in the 1850s, Italian patriots began a movement to win freedom which was called *Risorgimento*, "Rising Again." Its leaders were Giuseppe Mazzini and Count Camillo di Cavour. Without a strong army, these clever men had to use their wits. Count Cavour, the prime minister of Sardinia, gained the support of France against Italy's Austrian rulers.

In 1860 Giuseppe Garibaldi, the greatest hero of modern Italy, landed in Sicily with one thousand red-shirted volunteers. Fighting bravely, they drove out the foreign rulers and their armies. At last the new Kingdom of Italy was formed. Its first king, Victor

Emmanuel II, was crowned in 1861. Ten years later, the region that had belonged to the popes was added to the kingdom.

The new nation had many problems. It had large debts from the war of independence but had few resources to pay for them. While the people in the south were poor, Italy's rulers were mostly northerners. Their laws favored the north and hurt the south. The southerners, who had fought hardest for freedom, grew angry, and in some places they rose up against the northern rulers.

As time passed, Italy solved some of its problems. Industries rose in the north. From the south, millions of people left by ship for a better life in new lands. Four million of them went to America from 1880 until World War I. In 1915 Italy entered the war on the side of the Allies—France, Great Britain, and Russia.

The war was won, but it caused hard times afterward. Strikes and riots tore Italy apart, and a violent group led by Benito Mussolini took over the country. His bands of toughs, called Blackshirts, were able to keep order by force. Mussolini, who was known as *Il Duce* ("The Leader"), used terror and secret police to crush those who opposed him. His harsh method of rule, called fascism, ended many freedoms.

Mussolini did some good in Italy, and he was

Like this shepherd, most southern Italians made a hard living by farming or herding animals. Much of what they earned had to be paid to rich landowners.

liked by some of the people. Most Italians, however, didn't trust him or his plans to bring back Rome's past glory. Dreaming of a new empire, Mussolini ordered Italian troops to invade some weak African nations. Later he became an ally of Adolf Hitler, the warlike German leader who set out to conquer the world. Though his army was not ready, Mussolini led Italy into World War II on the losing side.

The Italian people suffered much in this unwanted war. Many were not sorry when the tide turned against Italy. They arrested Mussolini and asked for peace. But Hitler's soldiers freed Mussolini and moved into Italy. The Italians joined the Allies in driving them out. When they caught Mussolini a second time, they shot him.

After the war, Italy was a ruined country. The bombs and soldiers had destroyed many cities, and millions of people were hungry and homeless.

American aid helped the Italians make their country work again. Ruined cities, factories, and railroads were rebuilt. On June 2, 1946, Italy voted to become a republic. Under its new government, the lawmakers in the parliament are elected by the people, and the premier heads the government. Fifteen judges make up the Italian "Supreme Court."

For almost twenty-five years after the war, Italy grew rapidly. By 1970, though, the fast growth had slowed, and the country faced higher prices, fewer jobs, and unrest among the workers. Pollution and violence became serious problems.

Dangerous people, some calling themselves the Red Brigades, tried to change the country by force. These terrorists opposed all political parties. An official report in 1974 said that a terrorist bombing took place every sixty-seven hours, a kidnapping every five days, and a murder every nine hours. One recent victim was former premier Aldo Moro, who was kidnapped and killed by the Red Brigades. On May 13, 1981, a member of another terrorist group gravely wounded Pope John Paul II.

Even more dangerous than the Red Brigades are the gangsters of the Mafia. These secret clans, or close-knit groups, make enormous sums of money from organized crime. In fact, the Italian government estimates that the Mafia takes in $6 billion each year from supplying drugs such as heroin to buyers in the United States.

Gang wars between Mafia clans have resulted in many brutal killings. In the last three years, more than one thousand people have been killed. Recently these gangsters have attacked a number of government leaders who tried to put an end to their criminal activities. Sicilian Mafia clans have killed all the top state officials on the island who opposed them.

Former premier Aldo Moro was kidnapped and killed by the Red Brigades.

Former Premier Giovanni Spadolini expressed the alarm of many Italians when he said: "The Mafia has challenged the state, and the [survival] of the republic is at stake." The premier asked the Italian parliament to pass tougher laws to stop organized crime. Recently the parliament made membership in a Mafia clan a crime. It also gave special powers to law enforcement officials to investigate suspected Mafia members. The government believes that unless the Mafia is brought under control, it may become more powerful than the government itself.

Italy has had a difficult time dealing with its problems because its governments have not gained enough support to stay in power for long. Eight political parties hold blocks of seats in parliament. Those from the "left" and "right" disagree strongly. The Italian Communist Party, which is not connected with the Soviet Union, has received more votes than any other party except the Christian Democrats.

Italians are determined to solve their problems peaceably. Led by the Christian Democrats, the moderate parties have kept control. They are working hard to improve the economy. The Italian Communists have called for a new government in which they would share power with the Christian Democrats. Since the late 1970s, though, the Communists have lost some of their support. They have not become part of the nation's government.

In spite of high prices and weak governments, the Italian people are better off than they were in the past. They enjoy cars, televisions, telephones, and leisure time. The people of the south are no longer so poor that they must leave their country to go to other lands. Today, too, Italy is no longer divided and ruled by foreigners. It is a united country with a rich past, at peace with the other nations of the world.

4. Stories, Saints, and Sayings

Over their long past, Italians have learned much about the world. Until recent times, though, most workers and farmers could not read or write. Their wisdom was saved in folktales. These old stories about kings, fairies, magic animals, and ordinary people come from every part of the land.

Folktales are still told today in Italy. Often an old woman in a village has learned them by heart, and she passes them on to the young children. Their clever twists and lessons make them hard to forget.

Some folktales make fun of people who are lazy, proud, or stubborn. Here is one that is told in Sicily.

There was once a husband and wife who were both tailors. One day the husband came home and found some pots and plates broken in the kitchen. He was surprised because his wife was a good house-keeper. "How did these things get broken?" he cried.

The wife was busy cutting cloth with the scissors. "I don't know," she shrugged.

The husband kept demanding to know how the things were broken. At last the wife snapped at him, "I broke them—with these scissors!"

"With the scissors?" The husband wouldn't

accept this silly answer. "Come, how did you really break them?"

The wife was just as stubborn. "With the scissors!" was the only answer she would give.

The husband lost his temper. He took his wife outside, tied a rope around her, and began lowering her into the well. "Now you'll tell me!" he cried.

But the wife wouldn't give in. "It was the scissors!" she shouted.

The husband let her into the water up to her waist.

"It was the scissors," she called up.

He let her down till the water reached her chin.

"The scissors! The scissors!" she screamed.

The husband let the rope go. His wife sank under the water. She couldn't speak anymore, but she stuck her hand out of the water. With her fingers, she made the sign of cutting with the scissors!

The husband had no choice but to pull her out of the well. How the things were broken, he never learned. His wife had proved she was more stubborn than he.

Another folktale from the northern region of Friuli teaches a lesson about riches and happiness.

Long ago, a king had a son whom he loved dearly. But this young prince was always sad. The king tried every way to make him happy. He gave him costly gifts and fancy parties, but nothing worked. Even the prettiest maid in the kingdom couldn't make the poor prince smile.

At last the king's wise men came up with a plan. "You must search the kingdom for a happy man, Majesty. When you've found one who's truly happy, exchange the prince's shirt with his. That is the only way to help your son."

The king had his men search far and wide throughout his kingdom. First a very happy priest was brought to the king. "Would you like to be a bishop?" the king asked slyly.

"Yes, bless you, Majesty!" the priest answered.

The king sent him away in a rage. "I need a man who's happy as he is!"

Then a rich man was brought before the king. He had a good wife, many children, farms, sheep, and no enemies. He was kindly, and everyone said he was truly happy. "But when I go to bed at night, I can't sleep," he told the king. "I know that when I die, I'll have to leave everything."

He, too, was sent home with his shirt. Ready to give up, the king went out hunting alone. Far out in the fields, he heard a man singing. "Someone who sings like that must be truly happy," he thought. He quickly found him, working in the sunshine.

"Isn't it a beautiful morning, Majesty?" the man said as he trimmed the grapevines.

"A truly happy man at last! Would you like to come and live a life of ease with me in the palace?"

"No thanks, Majesty, I'm happy as I am. I wouldn't change places with anyone."

Now the king was sure he'd found his man. "Thank heaven!" he said. "But do me one favor, to save my own son." He hurried over to take the man's shirt. He unbuttoned the jacket—but then he gasped and let his arms drop.

The happy man was too poor to wear a shirt!

Italian children learn lessons from legends as well as folktales. Legends are stories from the past about real people and imaginary heroes. A number of them deal with Saint Peter, a companion of Jesus. In the stories, Peter is often lazy, greedy, or dishonest. Jesus makes him ashamed, and then forgives him.

In one legend from Palermo, Jesus was walking with his companions in the country. They were hungry, but there was no place for them to get bread. "Each man pick up a stone," Jesus said. All the men except Peter put heavy stones on their shoulders. Lazy Peter picked up the smallest stone he could find.

When they stopped to rest, Jesus prayed and the stones turned to bread. Peter's loaf, however, was as small as a roll! When he complained, Jesus scolded: "Why did you pick up such a small stone?"

The next day, Jesus again told the men to pick up

stones. This time Peter picked up a boulder he could hardly carry. The others chose small stones. "Let's have a joke on Peter," Jesus whispered. Before long they came to a town filled with bakeries and hot bread. Laughing, the men threw away their stones. At last Peter came huffing up with his boulder. When he saw all the bread, he was so angry that he couldn't eat!

Italy has always had its poor people, and some legends tell of the cruelty of the rich towards those who have little. From Sardinia comes the story of Fra Ignazio. This good man used to beg in the streets for the holy monks of Cagliari. His bed still stands in the monastery there.

Ignazio always begged from the poor, since they gave happily. He stayed away from the stingy lawyer Franchino because this man had become rich by cheating the poor.

One day Franchino complained to the head of the monks: "Why should Ignazio pass me by? Aren't I important, too?"

The head of the monks told Ignazio to beg from the thieving lawyer. He obeyed, and Franchino filled his sacks with costly goods.

But as Ignazio returned homeward, drops of blood began falling from the sacks. "A lucky day!" people called to him. "Ignazio has got some meat for the monks."

The monks came out to greet him. "We shall have fresh meat today!" they said happily. They opened the sacks—and found no meat inside. "But what about all that blood?" they cried, frightened.

Ignazio calmed them. "The blood came from the sacks all right," he said. "You see, the goods Franchino gave me are not his own. They are the blood of the poor people he has cheated."

Ignazio never again begged from the lawyer.

Some of Italy's best-loved legends deal with the saints. Saint Nicola, whom we call Santa Claus, is honored in the city of Bari. He started the custom of giving gifts in secret. One story tells how Saint Nicola came to the aid of three young sisters.

The girls' father was too poor to provide the gifts needed for his daughters to marry. Sadly, he decided to sell them so that they would not go hungry. Nicola, who was wealthy, heard of their trouble and went at night to their house. Through the window he tossed a bag of gold for the first daughter. The next night, he tossed a second bag.

On the third night, the father was waiting for him. He caught Nicola's arm and tried to thank him, but Nicola made him promise to keep his secret. He tossed the third bag and slipped away.

Saint Nicola was not an Italian. He was a bishop in Asia Minor, where he died in A.D. 326. Nine hundred years later, invaders were about to rob his tomb. Brave Italian sailors from Bari saved his body and brought it to their city. Today, in Bari, the people celebrate this rescue every May 7 and 8. They carry Nicola's statue, dressed in gold and red, to the waterfront. Singing and chanting, they place it on a flower-covered boat. Other boats follow it out to sea. At night, amid fireworks, the statue is brought back to Nicola's tomb.

Saint Rosalia is the patron saint of Palermo in Sicily. As a girl, she left a good home to live a life of prayer in a cave. She died there in 1160. One legend tells of Rosalia's great powers of holiness.

In 1664, when a sickness was killing thousands in Palermo, a lone hunter climbed nearby Mount Pellegrino. Rosalia appeared to him and asked what was happening in the city. "The people are falling like ripe pears," he said.

Rosalia told him where to find her bones. If these were brought to the city, she said, the sickness would end. The hunter, however, would die three days later.

The brave hunter did as he was told, and the sickness ended. Three days later, he died.

Today, on July 15, Rosalia's coffin is carried through Palermo on a huge golden chariot. A path has been built to her cave on the mountain. All year long, people come there to honor her.

One of Italy's most popular saints is Saint Francis of Assisi. Francis was born rich but gave all he had to the poor. Afterwards he lived a life of holiness. One legend tells how he saved the town of Gubbio from a wolf.

The wolf lived in a nearby forest. First it killed the people's cattle, and then it killed two men. The townspeople were so scared that they locked themselves in their homes.

Francis decided to go into the woods to deal with the wolf. He took no weapons with him because he knew the wolf must be old and hungry. Besides, Francis had a way with animals.

When Francis met the wolf, he began talking to it. The wolf listened. Francis promised that the wolf would be fed if it would stop killing. The wolf gave Francis its paw!

Francis led the wolf tamely into the town. The people came out of their homes in surprise. From that time on, they fed the wolf every day as it went from house to house like a beggar. Two years later, the gentle wolf died of old age.

Besides legends and tales, Italians are fond of proverbs. These are sayings which often contain a truth learned the hard way. For example, in the south people say, "Flies don't get into a closed mouth." They mean that you should keep quiet and mind your business, for then nothing unpleasant can happen to you. This is the wisdom of people who lived for ages under stern rulers. Those who spoke unwisely paid a heavy price—perhaps their lives.

Sometimes proverbs make clever rhymes in Italian speech: "*Unni rina, unni farina.*" This Sicilian saying means, "In some places sand, in some places flour." In other words, some people must live with nothing, while others are rich. Another one is, "*Prima il dovere, poi il piacere.*" This rhyme means "Duty first, then pleasure." It comes from the north, where many proverbs have to do with work and success. A favorite northern one is, "The large fish isn't caught on land." In other words, you must use your wits and take risks to get what you want.

Rest, food, and fun are important, too. Sometimes northerners remind themselves to enjoy their free time. "God helps a happy people," they say. A proverb from central Italy shares the same wisdom: "One does not grow old at the table." That is, we should not hurry the pleasures of eating and talking at meals.

From Sicily comes another saying about food: "The picky horse dies thin." This saying means that you should take what's offered, since you may not get anything else. It has to do with other things, too, such as choosing a husband or wife.

Another wise proverb is meant for new husbands: "A wife is like a brand new jewel-sack. What you save there, you always get back." In other words, in return for his kindness and respect, a man will have a loving wife. But the bad parts of husbands, wives, and friends also rub off: "He who lives with a lame person begins to limp at the end of a year." Without realizing it, this proverb says, we become like the people we choose to be with.

Often parents use sayings to teach their children what to value in life: "Honor is the poor man's treasure." And can you imagine a stern father reminding his child, "A clear sky fears no thunder"? That is, if your conscience is clear, you needn't fear punishment.

Proverbs like these are heard everywhere in Italy. The wisdom of the past is still carried on in folktales and legends. Of course, movies and TV have become more and more popular in recent years. And children enjoy reading fine stories like *Pinocchio*, which was written by an Italian, Carlo Collodi, in 1880. But the fondness for the spoken word has not died. Young and old still like to hear—and tell—a good story.

5. Holiday Fun

Italy is a land that is rich in holidays. Italians celebrate the usual Roman Catholic holy days, such as Christmas and Easter, and they also enjoy holidays for special saints. Most Italian cities and towns honor their patron saints with feasts, too. Throughout the year, holidays and festivals are times for rich foods, gifts, and fun.

The Christmas season is an especially happy time. On the nine nights before Christmas, families attend church services and sing the songs of the season. By Christmas Eve, a tiny Bethlehem scene, the *presepio*, has been set up in most homes. It has clay figures of the baby Jesus, or "Bambino," his mother Mary, the Madonna, and Saint Joseph, Mary's husband. Shepherds, kings, and animals also surround the Bambino.

Some of these scenes are very pretty and detailed. They have trees, grass, huts, glass ponds, and angels hung from wires. A fine presepio may have been handed down from parent to child. Its figures may be works of art.

Churches, too, set out large, fancy presepios. Many have hundreds of figures in colorful costumes.

A life-size presepio *in the Piazza Navona in Rome. The pipers in traditional costumes are called* Zampognari.

In some towns the churches compete for the best presepio, and children go from church to church to see them all. The first presepio may have been built by Saint Francis of Assisi more than seven hundred years ago. Today these beautiful scenes have come to stand for Christmas in Italy.

In some homes families gather before the prese-pio each morning to light candles and offer prayers. On Christmas Eve, the children recite poems that they have learned secretly. Later in the evening, families sit down for a special meal. In the north *cappelletti*, little dough "hats" stuffed with meat, is a favorite dish. In the south macaroni is often followed by roast chicken or meat in jelly. Around Rome the old custom was to serve a big cooked eel, called *capitone*. Today this custom is not as widely observed as it once was.

Special desserts are made for the Christmas Eve dinner. *Panettone* is a Christmas cake filled with candied fruit. *Cannoli*, cheese-filled pastries, *torrone*, nougat candy, and *panforte*, nut-filled gingerbread, are also served at this meal.

Afterward most Italian families go to church for Midnight Mass, which may be followed by torchlight parades for the Bambino. In the south the bagpipers who have come down from the hills play their Christmas music. The simple songs sound like lullabies. In some towns the Christmas sermon is given by a young boy. The one who is chosen earns a great honor.

Christmas Day is spent peacefully. Families may go visiting or have guests. The bustle of opening presents is not quite so great as in North America because only in recent years have many Italians exchanged gifts on Christmas morning. Christmas trees and Santa Claus are also rather new. The old custom was for simple gifts to be given to small children and old people on Christmas Eve. The real day for gift-giving was always January 6. This feast, the Epiphany, honors the Three Wise Men who gave gifts to the baby Jesus.

The wise men, though, do not leave the presents for Italian children—*la Befana*, the good witch, does. Her name comes from *l'Epifania*, Epiphany. Legends say that Befana was sweeping her house when the Wise Men passed by. They invited her to go with them to Bethlehem. Befana answered that she must finish her housework first. Later she took her broom and set out to find the Bambino. But she lost her way, and she has been searching for him ever since.

At Christmastime Befana appears in many Italian towns. A man dressed as an old woman plays her part. He wears a false hook nose, a shawl, a bandanna, and earrings.

In Rome children may visit Befana at a splendid toy fair. Hundreds of fun-filled toy stalls are set up in a big town square, or *piazza*, called the Piazza Navona. All over the square are balloons, fresh candy, hot food, and happy crowds. Young people blow toy whistles, horns, and cardboard trumpets while parents, grandparents, and friends gossip and buy toys. In the center are little houses for Befana, Santa Claus, and the Wise Men. Children visit them to talk about the toys they want.

Other children write letters to Befana as January 6 draws near. At last, down the chimney she comes on her broom, stuffing toys and candy into the stockings or shoes. Naughty children get stones or ashes. But the kindly Befana always leaves a real gift for them, too.

Not long after Epiphany, the season of *Carnevale* begins. This word means "farewell to meat." Carnevale is a time of feasting and fun just before the fasting season of Lent when people go without some foods.

Carnevale season begins January 17 and lasts several weeks. Long ago, people made merry for all those weeks. Today, though, the real fun takes place on the last three days. The Tuesday before Ash Wednesday, *Martedi Grasso*, is the gayest. There are parades, plays, and music all through Italy. Townspeople crowd into the streets to dance, eat, and have fun. Confetti fills the air, and paper streamers hang everywhere.

Each town has its own festival. In some, big, fancy floats carrying people in fantastic costumes are pulled through the streets. Some floats are as big as houses or boats.

Other towns enjoy bands, singers, acrobats, or a Parade of the Months. In this parade, the months are men dressed in special costumes. They sing songs to the Carnevale King, who is made up as a great, fat man because Carnevale is a time of feasting.

In Venice this fat king is a dummy filled with straw and firecrackers. After all the wild fun, he is set on fire at midnight of Martedi Grasso. The crowd cheers as he lights up the lovely Saint Mark's Square.

Young children especially like Carnevale. One reason is that many of them are given pretty costumes to wear. Another is that Carnevale is a time for pranks. In Rome young boys flock to Cola di Rienzo, a street set aside for the fun. They carry clubs of soft rubber to play a game in which they hit other boys on the head without being seen. The boys try to surprise, not hurt. After the game they eat candies, nuts, ice cream, and strangely-shaped animal cookies.

Soon after Carnevale comes another big feast, Saint Joseph's Day, on March 19. Saint Joseph was the husband of Mary, the Madonna. As the protector of the holy family, he has become the patron of orphans. His day is honored not only by feasting, but also by sharing with the poor.

That is why in Sicily a special outdoor meal is prepared. The villagers set up a banquet table called "Saint Joseph's table." They collect money, food, and flowers to prepare the feast, and all kinds of tasty dishes are set on the big table. Then, after morning mass, the banquet begins. Widows, orphans, beggars, and all the needy are welcomed. The people sing, dance, and light bonfires to honor Saint Joseph.

An Italian feast is not complete without fireworks. One famous display takes place each year in Florence on the day before Easter. It's called *Scoppio del Carro*, or "Explosion of the Car."

For two days before, everything is sad and quiet in the churches. For Christians, these days stand for the time the dead Jesus spent in the tomb. The statues are covered, and no bells ring.

But at noon of Holy Saturday, the joy of his rising begins. The churchbells ring for the Mass of Glory. Thousands crowd into the piazza before the cathedral of Holy Mary of the Flower. White oxen pull a big, fancy wooden cart up to the church doors. This is the Carro, loaded with fireworks. A wire joins it to the high altar inside the church.

At last the Mass ends, and the crowd outside grows excited. Suddenly a rocket shaped like a dove is lit at the altar. It shoots along the wire and through the doors of the church to the Carro. With a terrific noise, the Carro explodes! The crowd cheers. The Lord has risen from the dead, and the sad time is over!

*A huge crowd watches the Carro explode before the cathedral
of Holy Mary of the Flower in Florence.*

On Ascension Day, forty days after Easter,
another noisy feast is held in Florence. Ascension
Day is a spring holiday when many Italian families go
on picnics. But in Florence they go to Cascine Park
for the *Festa del Grillo*, the Cricket Festival.

Just like the first robins, the crickets' singing is a happy sign of spring. Days before the feast, children buy little wicker cages. Then they hunt for crickets. Crickets that sing are thought to bring the family good luck for the coming year. Males are prized as the best singers. But how can you tell a male cricket from a female? A tiny yellow stripe around its neck is the clue.

On the day of the Cricket Festival, children proudly carry their crickets to Cascine Park. Parents bring along picnic lunches. At the park vendors sell caged crickets, sweets, and colorful balloons. Children run about with their pretty painted cages, and everyone enjoys a day in the outdoors. Afterward the children free their crickets, for this is another way to bring good luck.

A belief in luck and miracles makes many Italian feasts richer. One such feast is held on Saint John's Day. John, the cousin of Jesus, was a fearless preacher who was killed by his enemies. On his feast day, June 24, some Italians get out of bed at sunrise. They say that you can see John's face lighting up the sky.

The feast of Saint Januarius on September 19 celebrates an event Italians believe is a miracle. Saint Gennaro, as Italians call him, is the patron of Naples. The Roman rulers put him to death long ago. Later, when his body and a jar holding his hardened blood were brought to Naples, an amazing thing happened. The blood turned soft again!

Now the softening of the blood is a special event in Naples each year. The saint's chapel is finely decorated. In the streets a lovely carpet of flower petals is laid. The crowd kneels in the chapel and watches for the blood to soften. The priest lifts up a jeweled stand holding the jar. "Do your miracle, little saint!" the people cry. The blood may take hours to soften. But if it softens quickly, it means a period of good luck.

Unlike other Italian cities, Siena has two special days each year. July 2 and August 16 are the days of the Palio, a famous horse race. Both races honor the Madonna.

Visitors crowd into Siena for the Palio. The city is divided into seventeen sections, each with an animal name such as Eagle, Snail, and Panther. Only ten horses enter the race because the cobbled course is so narrow. The course is two miles long, or three times around the main piazza. Mattresses guard the bad turns.

The ten horses are chosen by drawing lots. On the morning of the race, they are brought to church for a blessing. The brightly robed jockey and horse walk right up the red carpet to the altar.

Siena's people are very loyal to their sections of

the city. Husbands and wives who were born in different sections split up to cheer their horses. Children go with their mothers. The piazza, streets, and balconies are jammed, for everyone wants to see the dangerous race.

A parade starts the festival. Expert flag-tossers and knights in gleaming armor march through the crowded streets. Last come two white oxen pulling the prize cart. It holds the Palio, a black and gold silk banner with an image of the Madonna. Each section wants the honor of winning it.

When the parade is done, the cannon roars, and the race begins. As the horses race swiftly around the square, the jockeys lash each other with special whips. The crowd shouts and claps. Sometimes a horse stumbles or a jockey falls. At last one speeding rider flashes first across the finish line. His section cheers wildly and raises him on their shoulders. Both he and his horse are brought back to the church to give thanks. Then come music, dancing, and feasting far into the night.

Not all holidays are as festive as the Palio. November 2 is honored as The Day of the Dead. On this day families place flowers and candles on the graves of their dead.

Even this feast day, though, is not really sad. "Beans of the Dead," bean-shaped almond cakes, are

Horses race around a dangerous turn during the Palio in Siena.

eaten. Around Rome sweethearts announce their weddings, and in Sicily children enjoy a special treat. If they are good, and if they pray for the dead, they receive gifts. It is the dead, they are told, who bring the sweets and toys during the night.

Best of all, no sooner is the Day of the Dead finished than Christmas is near again. The calendar, with all its feasts, is about to start a new year once more.

6. *Pasta Power*

What foods come to mind when you think of Italian cooking? Macaroni? Pizza? Spaghetti and meatballs? These are a few of the "Italian" dishes Americans enjoy. But to Italians they are only a small part of a very rich menu.

"Bread and water is fit for a dog." This old Italian saying means that food for people should always be special. It should be tasty, varied, and pleasing to the eye. To Italians food is more than the fuel of life. It is also the soul of enjoyment, rest, and gatherings of people. In fact, it is a way of sharing happiness and love. "*Mangia!*" "Eat!" the mother urges her children. "*Mangia!*" the host says over and over to his guests.

Italian holidays would seem bare without fancy dishes. Roast baby lamb, roasted artichokes, and Easter broth are served for Easter. Special desserts are made for holy days. Italians really enjoy the food at fairs and feasts. Roast mutton chops are given out at the Mutton Chop Fair of Castel Saint Pietro. At the Ham Fair of Saint Daniele in Friuli, visitors receive free ham. Spaghetti is dished out at the Spaghetti Fair near Naples. Sharing food is a way of making people feel welcome.

An Italian family shares a meal at an outdoor restaurant.

Since good food is so important in an Italian home, a tasty meal is planned when guests are expected. The bustle of cooking fills the house.

Perhaps the main course will be *ravioli*, a pasta dish. If these small, filled balls of dough are to be homemade, the dough must be mixed and rolled flat. Fillings must be made, too. Ravioli are really dough pockets holding little mounds of spinach, cheese, or chopped meat. The dough is folded over the filling and pinched shut.

Cooking the ravioli is fun if everyone helps. The kitchen table is white with flour and dough. An older child trims the ravioli with a wiggly cutter wheel. On the stove, spices and meat simmer in a thick tomato sauce. Somewhere—perhaps on the beds—clean sheets are spread to dry the ravioli. The little children carry them from the kitchen, one in each hand. Trip after trip they make. Soon there are hundreds of little square pastas in neat rows.

The real fun begins when the guests arrive. Let's imagine a Sunday gathering of aunts, uncles, cousins, and grandparents. Everyone talks at once. As the pots of water boil, the children are sent to fetch the ravioli. The guests sit at the table, and *antipasto*, a platter of appetizers such as cold cuts, olives, peppers, and cheeses, is served. When the wine glasses are filled, even the children may have some.

Next come the boiled ravioli, topped with the delicious sauce. They are so good that everyone eats as many as possible. One cousin counts eighteen, and another, twenty-one. Seconds are dished out, and then thirds. An uncle eats thirty-eight ravioli! "Just one more," is heard around the table again and again.

Finally, everyone is stuffed, unless they have saved room for another course of meat or fish. Dessert—pastry, fruit, or ice cream—is still to come. Strong *espresso* coffee, figs, and nuts may be served, too. The children leave to play on their own, but the grown-ups sit and talk some more. After all, it will soon be time for another snack of leftovers!

Meals based on pasta are common in Italy. This "paste," or dough, is made from durum wheat. Since it is hard to knead, most people buy their pasta ready-made. Many Italians, though, still make their own. The dough can be cut into more than one hundred shapes. Each has a name and taste of its own.

Some of the names are clever reminders of the shapes. *Bucatini* are "little holes," *farfalle* are "butterflies," and *agnolotti* are "little fat lambs." *Tortellini* are "little twists." One legend claims that they were copied from the shape of the belly button of the goddess Venus. The long strands of pasta called spaghetti are well known to us. But how would you like to eat a plate of "little worms," "wolf's eyes," "snails," or "horse's teeth"? All are popular pasta shapes.

Pasta has been eaten in Italy for centuries. Once people believed that Marco Polo brought it there from China. But now we know that Sicilians invented it, and Neapolitans learned how to dry and store it. *Maccaruni* is mentioned in records that are seven hundred years old.

One old legend tells how an unpopular king first tasted pasta. He was invited to a Sicilian lord's house for dinner. When the meal was served, the pasta tubes were stuffed with soil instead of cheese. Calmly, the king said a prayer over the food. By a miracle, the soil became ricotta cheese. Today this dish is still a favorite in Catania, a large Sicilian city. Filled with ricotta and chopped meat, it is called *cannelloni*, or "big pipes."

This mixing of soft cheese and pasta makes a number of other tasty Italian dishes. Stuffed pasta shells called *manicotti* and baked *ziti* are examples. *Lasagna* is a rich dish of broad noodles, meatballs, sauce, and *mozzarella* cheese. Sliced egg, mushrooms, and vegetables may also be added. All are set in layers in a deep pan, and baked. Grated cheese and spices top this handsome pasta dish.

Tomato sauce is used in lasagna and many other Italian dishes. Even meat and eggplant dishes are baked in tomato sauce. From place to place, cooks prize the special flavors their spices add to the sauce. But it all starts with the tomato, a fruit that was brought to Italy from Peru in the 1500s. Today it is grown in every region of the country.

Other sauces are used, too. Fish sauce may have clams, squid, or anchovies mixed in, and a Sicilian version uses sardines, fennel, and breadcrumbs. One rich sauce is made with butter, cream, grated cheese, and bacon bits. It is usually poured over ribbon noodles called *fettucine*. An easy sauce can be made with oil and garlic. Even butter alone makes a tasty sauce. It is said that butter was invented in Lodi, near Milan. Before its good taste was noticed, it was used as body grease!

Now that you have learned about pasta and sauces, you may want to make a pasta dish for your family or friends. Spaghetti with butter is an easy one. Bring a large pot of lightly salted water to a boil. Open a one-pound box of number eight or nine spaghetti and drop about one-third of the noodles at a time into the water. You may want to break them in half first. Stir a few times to keep the noodles from sticking. Boil them with the lid off for about ten minutes. Then sample one noodle to make sure it is *al dente*, "firm to the tooth." The noodles should not be boiled so long that they become very soft.

Next, pour the spaghetti into a colander to drain the water and place it in a serving bowl. Add butter, garlic powder, and pepper. With a little grated cheese, you have a delicious pasta dish for four.

In the north of Italy, people eat more rice and corn than pasta. Italians use ground corn to make a puddinglike dish called *polenta*. Polenta can be boiled, fried, roasted, or toasted, and it goes well with fish, meat, or sauce. One popular dish in Friuli in the northeast is a mixture of polenta and little birds.

Another is polenta and *bacalà*, or dried salt cod that has been simmered in milk, oil, onions, and spices.

Two other starchy foods, bread and potatoes, form an important part of the diet of many Italians. Potatoes are often made into *gnocchi*. These are small balls of mashed potato and flour, quickly boiled. Italian breads take many shapes. In the Piedmont of the northwest, crisp bread sticks are eaten. In the south Calabrians bake huge round loaves which weigh as much as twenty pounds. They also make colored breads called *pitte*. Sardinians like large, soft loaves and paper-thin bread known as "sheet music."

These starchy foods are important in a land where beef and fish are costly. One tasty Italian beef dish is Florentine beefsteak. Alpine trout also make a fine meal. But pork, veal, chicken, sausages, and cold cuts like salami and Parma ham are the most common. From the town of Busseto comes a fine, spicy ham called *culatelli*. Only a few families know the secret of making it. One step is to give the hams rubdowns as they cure.

In addition to meat, pasta, and other filling foods, Italians eat vegetables of all kinds. Tomatoes, lettuce, and peppers add a touch of class to almost any meal. Many Italians grow their own greens in kitchen gardens. Some cooks go to great trouble to get what they need. Truffles, wild mushroomlike plants which grow under the soil, add a delicious flavor to foods. But they are very hard to find. Truffle hunters use trained dogs to sniff them out. They work at night to keep their favorite spots secret.

Italian cheeses and soups also add variety to meals. *Gorgonzola* is a world famous cheese that is often served as a dessert. *Minestrone* is a thick soup filled with beans, greens, and tomatoes. *Brodetto* is one of many rich fish soups. In some places a sea stone is boiled with the soup to add just the right flavor.

In Italy no main meal would be complete without wine. Since tap water is often not good for drinking, having good table wines is important for human health. That's why children, too, are given wine and coffee as well as soft drinks.

Italian coffee is made strong from freshly ground beans. It is drunk in several ways. *Caffelatte*, "coffee-milk," is an even mixture of coffee and hot milk which is served with rolls or pastry for breakfast. Coffee mixed with water is called *caffe lungo*, "long" or thinned coffee. *Cappucino* is coffee with just a little milk that has the light brown color of a Capuchin monk's cloak. Coffee is also drunk black, with sugar, most often at dinner time. This main meal is served early in the afternoon, usually after one o'clock. A smaller meal is eaten late in the evening.

Children help harvest grapes for wine making in the Tuscany region north of Rome.

One Italian dish, pizza, is a late evening snack or meal for many young people in North America. In Italy this flat bread pie is topped with mozzarella cheese, tomato sauce, and chunks of meat or fish to make a cheap and wholesome meal. Sicilians make a thick pizza topped with onions. Genoese pizza is made with anchovies, garlic, and black olives.

The thin pizza of Naples is sold in shops as a hot snack. It can be topped with all kinds of tasty tidbits, and people munch it as they walk down the street. Folded in half like a purse, it is called a *libretto*, a "little book." "Passtimes" are also sold in Naples.

Eating pizza, Neapolitan style. Naples is known for its many pizza shops.

These are tiny pizzas, or small helpings of seafood or vegetables.

Italians enjoy many other hot snacks. One treat is a small pie of pasta dough filled with cheese or onions. Another is a hot mozzarella sandwich, which is a dish you may want to make yourself. Place a few slices of mozzarella cheese between two slices of bread. Coat the sandwich in a mixture of beaten egg and breadcrumbs. Then fry it in olive oil. Delicious!

In Italian cities people buy hot snacks from push-carts and stalls. Snails and octopus are popular. Boiled beans or chickpeas, sausages, and chestnuts are enjoyed by many city people, too. In Sicily pig, goat, and calf innards are made into tasty snacks.

Italians also like such sweet snacks as rice cakes, marzipan, and ices. In Tuscany vendors sell spicy, waferlike pastries and chestnut-flour cakes topped with raisins and pine nuts.

Italian children like desserts, whether plain or fancy. Fresh fruit or melon often ends a meal. Sometimes *spumoni*, rich ice cream, is served, or a pudding made with eggs, sugar, and wine. *Mostaccioli* are honey cookies spread with icing and cut in the shapes of animals or saints. Cooks in Abruzzo make a soft cake topped with chocolate.

Some desserts are made especially for holidays. On Easter children get small, ring-shaped breads baked with Easter eggs in the center. Special Christmas fruitcakes are served in every region. The Milanese type is the most popular. Another Christmas cake, *panforte*, is made with almonds, cocoa, fruit, hazelnuts, and spices. *Cullurelli* are deep-fried Christmas pastries made of flour and mashed potato and sprinkled with powdered sugar.

One very fancy Italian dessert, "English Soup," is a rum layer cake filled with custard and whipped cream. Sicilian desserts often use candied fruit, ice cream, and nuts. Sicilian Cake is made with ricotta cheese, chocolate, cherries, and fruit.

From appetizers to desserts, Italian cooking has something for every taste. Since the time of the Romans, new dishes have been added from around the world. Sherbet, marzipan, and sugar came from the Arab lands. Potatoes, corn, and tomatoes came from the New World. In turn, Italians shared their ways of preparing food. The first cookbook was written by Bartolomeo Sicci, an Italian, in 1474. Since then the give and take has never stopped. No wonder there are so many delicious Italian foods today.

7. *School Days*

Italians are proud that their country offers free education to all young people. All children from six to fourteen years old must go to school. Nearly nine out of ten students attend free public schools.

In some ways school in Italy is different than it is in North America. For example, Italian children wear uniforms and go to school on Saturdays. Often students have no playgrounds or school sports. Young children don't eat lunch in school, either, because their school day ends at 12:30. In Italy all of the time spent in school is devoted to schoolwork. Games, sports, and friends must wait until afterward.

A child's schooling often starts at the age of three or four with a kindergarten or a private nursery school. The nursery schools care mainly for children of working or pregnant mothers.

At age six, *scuola elementare*, or grade school, begins. A very bright child may skip first grade and start in second. The grade school is usually a small school of about one hundred thirty boys and girls. Each class has only one teacher for all subjects, and sometimes this teacher stays with the class through several grades.

Students in a classroom in the village of Cori.

After five years, students who plan to go on to college enter *scuola media,* "middle school." Scuola media is like a three-year American junior high school. Boys and girls may have a different teacher for each subject, and lessons commonly last one hour. Students who don't plan to attend college go to a vocational school instead of the scuola media. They learn skills that will help them find jobs when they finish their training.

Many scuola media students go on to a higher

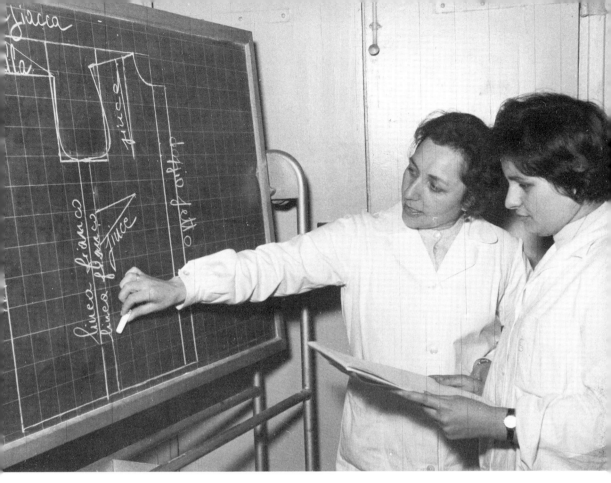

A lesson at a professional training school in Genoa.

school called a *liceo*. To enter it they must pass a government test. When they finish their studies at the liceo, they must take another exam to go on to college.

There are several types of liceos. The classical liceo offers Latin, Greek, and other subjects leading to college. The scientific liceo prepares young people for careers in science. Both last five years. The artistic liceo is a four-year music and arts school where students learn painting, sculpture, and music along with other subjects.

Young people who wish to become teachers go to schools which lead to teacher training college. Graduates of vocational schools may attend five-year technical and trade schools. Each offers special training for jobs in particular fields: farming, business, mining, metal work, shipbuilding, and textiles.

Other young people, mostly boys, become apprentices. They go to work for carvers, weavers, glass blowers, and other craftsmen. These boys are taught the masters' skills and secrets. After years of hard work, they will be craftsmen themselves.

Many students from the liceos continue their schooling in one of Italy's more than thirty colleges and universities. The University of Bologna, begun in 1088, is the oldest in Europe. Most of these schools are run by the Italian government. In the past they served only the best students. Today, however, they are open to a great number of young people. The University of Rome, for example, has ten times as many students as it did a few years ago.

Let's imagine what a day in an Italian grade school would be like. The children gather outside the school gate at about quarter-past eight in the morning. Some have come to school on buses, while others have walked or ridden bicycles. Along the grey wall are stands for parking bikes.

The children are noisy and excited. Boys line up

on one side, girls on the other. That is a rule in this school.

Both boys and girls wear uniforms. Their pretty blue smocks reach almost to the knee. These easy-to-care-for garments are practical as well as charming. They have wide, white collars with big red bows at the throat. The class badge is worn on one sleeve, and some children have their initials embroidered on their smocks. Most carry their books in knapsacks over their shoulders.

Just before half-past eight, a teacher comes to open the gate. The students file in, a bit noisily but not rudely. The school has a small courtyard, but no playground. Inside are seven classrooms, a common room, a teachers' room, and some offices. This school does not have a gym, a library, or a theater. It is a place of classrooms, students, and teachers.

In one classroom the teacher is a little late. The two dozen children hang their knapsacks on hooks attached to their desks. They talk and relax. When the teacher enters the room, they all stand quietly. This sign of respect is a custom in Italian schools.

The teacher, a man of middle age, waves at them to sit down. He has a moustache and gentle, smiling eyes. While his voice can be sharp at times, the students like him.

The first hour is a lesson about Italian history.

First, the class secretary reads his or her notes from the day before to remind the class of what they have learned. A different boy or girl has this job each week.

Today's lesson is about the *Risorgimento*, Italy's rise to freedom. The teacher talks of Mazzini, Count Cavour, and Garibaldi. The students listen and take notes. Their notebook pages are lined like graph paper because the squares help them to write letters neatly. From time to time the students raise their hands to ask questions. To the teacher's questions, they answer freely. They call their teacher *maestro*, or "master."

Partway through the lesson, the teacher pulls down a movie screen and uses a slide projector to show pictures. All the students know Garibaldi's face. But who is that man with the soft white hair? "George Washington," the maestro explains. He shows pictures of Thomas Jefferson and Simón Bolívar, too, for this lesson is about how countries around the world gained their freedom.

Next comes a math lesson. The teacher takes out a big bundle of sticks and groups them by tens. One girl is chosen to be his helper. Together they show how multiplying is just a fast way of adding. Six bundles make sixty sticks. "Are you sure? Why not count them?" says the maestro. After all the sticks have been counted, the answer is still sixty. The students groan when the teacher gives them multiplying problems for homework.

When the class gets too restless, the maestro picks up his guitar and starts playing. It's rest time! A few children take out recorders and join in the song. The others listen or stretch their legs.

The third lesson of the day is writing. The students take out note paper and get to work on their poems and stories about women in history. The teacher has talked about women leaders, artists, and authors. Now the students are imagining what it would be like to meet them.

Three children are writing about Maria Montessori, the first woman in Italy to become a doctor. This remarkable woman started schools for poor children. Her revolutionary method of teaching was based on children's natural interests. Today this famous "Montessori method" is used in many countries.

The story of Maria Montessori and other student writings will be bound into a little magazine with drawings and a pretty cover. Many schools have been making these magazines for years. Some share ideas on making school life more fun, while others print the honor roll.

The children don't do their writing projects in silence. Some talk, and some walk from desk to desk. The noise they make is a good noise of people working. If it gets too loud, the teacher makes a sharp hissing sound to quiet them.

Finally, the third lesson is done. Before this school day ends, the students are putting on a play written by two classmates. Every child has a part. The maestro's guitar is needed, too, for the play has songs. After much talk about who should do what, the children are eager to begin. The play is acted out, and everyone has fun.

At half-past noon, the dismissal bell ends the day. The students pack their knapsacks, bid the maestro good-bye, and march out through the gate. School is over, but there is a long afternoon ahead.

Older students in a scuola media have more subjects to learn than grade school students. They study the Italian language and literature, geography, science, civics, and a foreign language. They also learn a little about music, art, and religion. In addition, some students practice handicrafts such as woodworking or pottery.

In most middle schools, young people go on lengthy field trips. Often they travel to nearby big cities where they may stay two or three days. They go to plays, concerts, museums, and libraries.

Students in scuola medias and other schools have problems because many school buildings are old, and some have little equipment. In fact, many middle schools do not have a science lab. In the poor areas of the south, some schools are shabby, indeed. On the other hand, many, new, well-equipped schools have been built in recent years.

One problem that most Italian schools do not have is bad behavior by students. Most children are polite, and bullying is rare. Not much time is spent in school except in classes. There are rules, of course, for absence, for care of desks, and for use of bathrooms. Students are punished for bad manners or vulgar words. Most punishments, though, are light.

The good behavior of Italian students may be due in part to the strict grading and testing system in their schools. Usually young people take exams in June before they are allowed to pass on to the next grade. For those who fail this exam, another one is given in September. Students who fail both exams have to repeat their grade.

At the end of the school year, some schools give prizes to outstanding students. Medals, books, and even prize money are awarded. Proud parents some-times buy books for their children, too.

For good students and bad, Italian schools are places for serious study. Young people have fun, too, but they are never allowed to forget that school is a place for learning. Their teachers remind them that the right to an education is important to all Italians.

8. Sports for All Seasons

In every land, sports help people relax and have fun. Italians, too, are glad for a break from their jobs and schoolwork. They enjoy many games and sports.

Italy has a long coastline and mild weather. Since few Italians live very far from a beach, many of them enjoy water sports.

Imagine a bright sun on dazzling white sand. Colorful umbrellas and canvas windbreaks dot the beach. Children play with pails and shovels, and families unpack big picnic lunches. From the surf, shouts and cries ring out in several languages. Nearby, stalls sell hot food and cold drinks. Few things are more fun than a day at the beach!

Italy has fine swimming beaches all around its long coastline. In the northwest is the Italian Riviera, stretching west and east of Genoa. A little to the south are the sandy beaches of Forte dei Marmi and Viareggio. Directly across the country on the east coast is the famous resort of Rimini. Rimini has a boardwalk with shops, nightclubs, and beauty parlors.

At Ostia, near Rome, the sand is clean, and black. To the south lie Capri and Ischia, two island resorts near Naples which can be reached only by boat.

Sunbathers enjoy the bright sun and white sand of this beach on the island resort of Ischia near Naples.

Sicily's best beaches are at Mazzaro and Mondello. Most southern Italians, though, do not enjoy sunbathing because the summer sun is burning hot. By custom, people stop work and stay out of the heat at midday. They think that sitting uncovered at the beach is a crazy thing to do.

Besides swimming, many Italians enjoy skin diving and spearfishing near the islands of Ponza and Elba off of Italy's west coast. Water skiing is popular at Capri. On the pretty lakes of Como, Garda, and Maggiori in northern Italy, many speedboats race. Each year a famous regatta is held in Venice on the first Sunday of September. Throughout the warm weather months, people enjoy these water sports.

When winter comes, Italians take to the ski slopes. There are many charming ski resorts in the Alps and Dolomites. Some resorts have special mountain railways, called funiculars, and most have modern ski lifts and ski schools. They offer other winter sports, too, such as skating and bobsledding.

In parts of the north, skiing is year-round. In the south the season runs from Christmas until late March. Romans ski at resorts in the Abruzzi Mountains, which are less than three hours from the city by car. Sicilians ski on pretty Mount Etna. The busiest ski season is the Christmas holidays when thousands of Italians "hit the slopes." Children often go with

Skiers climb the slopes of Mount Etna in Sicily.

their parents, for even small children speed down the slopes with skill.

Summer and winter, the sport that most Italians enjoy is *calcio*, or soccer. It is said that if you toss a ball to an American child, he or she will hit it with a stick. An Italian child, however, will kick it. Like sandlot baseball in America, all that a soccer game takes is some children and some open space. Goal zones can be scratched onto the ground, sides chosen—and the game is on!

Some Italian children play especially hard

because they hope to play for a club team some day. There are more than six thousand soccer clubs in Italy. Still other children dream of becoming professional soccer players. Some of these players are paid large sums of money for signing with teams. They are like first-round draft picks in American sports.

In Italy soccer has more fans by far than any other sport. It's as popular as American football, baseball, basketball, and hockey put together. All large cities have soccer teams. People watch the matches closely on TV, and thousands cram into big stadiums to cheer for their teams.

Italian fans are very serious about the game. Their feelings run so strong that sometimes they get out of hand. Police must shield players who perform badly because the fans throw bottles, umbrellas, and fruit onto the field. Once fans chased a losing team right out of the stadium! But fans are just as free with their praise when their teams win. They treat star players like national heroes.

Throughout the year, Italian soccer stars play in tournaments in Italy and in other countries. One of the biggest tournaments is the Intercontinental Cup. In the finals, the best team from Europe faces the best South American team. They play a series of home and away games. The winner is called the world's best professional club team.

The most important soccer tournament of all is the World Cup. In this worldwide event, 130 nations compete for the title. Each country's team is made up of its best players, who are honored to be chosen to represent their country. The World Cup finals are held every four years, two years after the Olympic Games.

Since these matches are like the World Series, Super Bowl, and Stanley Cup combined, Italians follow them with great interest. Their team won the World Cup in 1934 and 1938. In 1970, though, Italy lost in the finals to Brazil. Pelé, the Brazilian superstar, beat Italy's famed defense, called *catenaccio*. Loyal Italian soccer fans were very sad.

In 1982, the Italians came back to win the World Cup a third time by defeating the West German team. Afterward, people danced in the streets all through Italy. Once more their team was the champion of the world.

Another sport with many fans in Italy is bicycle racing. Top cyclists are as famous and well paid as movie stars. The biggest race of the year is the Tour of Italy, which is held in the spring. This long-distance race starts in Milan and goes through much of the country. Hundreds of cyclists compete, and millions of people watch on TV.

An even longer race is the Tour of France. This

three-thousand-mile race starts in France but crosses into Italy and other countries. Cyclists must pedal over mountains and through cities and towns. There is a winner for each day or "stage." Trucks, vans, and cars carry the racers' supplies, and reporters, trainers, and judges travel along, too.

Winning the Tour of France is the highest honor in cycling. Fausto Coppi, an Italian, won it in 1949 and 1952. His time in 1949 was 149 hours, 40 minutes, and 49 seconds for pedaling 3008 miles! Another Italian, Felice Gimondi, was the winner in 1965.

Auto racing is nearly as popular in Italy as bike racing. The *Mille Miglia*, or "Thousand Miles," is the most famous race. Drivers come from all over the world to enter it. Held every April, the race uses regular roads. It starts at Brescia, a city in northern Italy, and from there the cars drive down the west coast and across the country toward Rome. Then they speed up the east coast and head inland back to Brescia for the finish. Race fans watch at different points along the course.

The Italian Grand Prix, another big auto race, takes place at Monza, near Milan. Grand Prix racing is for special "formula" cars that are required to have engines of a certain size. These streamlined race cars have single seats, open cockpits, roll bars, and special fuel tanks. For safety the drivers wear helmets, gog-

Some Italians can't wait to learn about cars and racing. These young people are learning to drive at a government run auto-driving school in a Rome park.

gles, and fireproof overalls. There are doctors at every corner of the course, and fire engines stand ready to speed to the scene of an accident. Driving at 200 miles per hour (302 kilometers per hour) is dangerous!

Grand Prix races are held in many countries. Since 1950, only these events have counted in the contest for the driver's World Championship. Giuseppe Farina, the first world champion, was an Italian. Albert Ascari, also of Italy, won in 1952 and 1953. Mario Andretti, an American racer who began his career in Italy, has become a Grand Prix star in recent years. In the United States he is known for his victory in the Indianapolis 500 auto race.

Just as Mario Andretti became well known in America, American athletes have become stars in Italy. Basketball has many fans in Italy, and the Italians have started their own basketball leagues. Their players, though, are not quite as good as those in America.

To improve their quality of play, the Italian leagues passed a rule that allowed each of the twenty-eight top Italian teams to hire one foreign player. These new players were nearly always Americans. The fans were so pleased with their higher level of play that the rule was changed to allow two foreign players per team. Coaches were sent to America to find tall centers and forwards.

The Americans are glad for the chance to play on a professional team. Many of them are athletes who were not able to play professional basketball in the United States. In Italy they play every game and are treated well by the fans. Most enjoy living among the Italian people, but they still find it strange to see Italian players kiss one another after a good play.

Italians who don't go to see basketball games may bet on them instead. Huge sums are bet each week in a government run soccer pool, and there are also betting pools for dog and horse racing. *Il Lotto* is the Italian national lottery. It's based on the game of lotto, which was invented more than three hundred years ago in Genoa.

The sports pools raise money for the Italian National Olympic Committee. Italy has sent many fine athletes to the Olympics. They often win medals in skiing, bobsledding, fencing, and tennis. In 1960, when Rome hosted the Olympic Games, many of the world's best athletes performed there. Four years earlier, the winter Olympics were held in Cortina.

Whether watching, betting, or playing, Italians can always fill their free time with a game. Card games are very popular. Bridge, canasta, *scopone*, and *briscola* are favorite card games.

Italians play another game, *morra*, with nothing but their fingers. Here's how it's played: Two players

The ice stadium for the 1956 winter Olympic Games in Cortina, Italy.

face each other and throw out any number of fingers on one hand. At the same moment, each calls out a number. If the number equals the total of fingers on the other player's hand, the player who said it wins.

Speed is what makes morra fun. Faster and faster come the fingers and the calls. Eyes dart, and minds strain. Without meaning to, the players start to shout. They throw their fingers like weapons. Soon they're roaring as if they were really fighting!

Bocce players don't get as excited as morra players do. Bocce, a game of wooden balls, is as old as ancient Rome. Once a sport for old men, it's now played by young people, too.

Bocce is played on a long, narrow cinder court. Teams can have from one to four players. Each team gets four grapefuit-size balls. One player rolls a special smaller ball called the *pallino*. Then the others roll their balls as close to it as they can. Skilled bocce players use angles and spins and bank shots off the wooden sides of the court.

A team wins points for every ball closer than the other team's nearest ball. Sometimes the best play is to knock away the other team's ball. A skilled player will launch the heavy ball high in the air. Down it comes, sixty feet away. Bang! It knocks away just one ball, leaves the pallino untouched, and its own backspin stops it in place. With this kind of action, it's not surprising to see many people stand watching at the bocce court. And young people like the game so much that they will pratice it for hours.

Bocce, soccer, cycling, swimming, skiing—Italians have sports and games for every part of the year. For rich and poor alike, these games and sports make Italy a fun place to live.

9. New Lives in a New Land

America is often called the great "melting pot" of immigrants. Since Columbus crossed the ocean five hundred years ago, a stream of newcomers has come to this vast land from every corner of the world. Many people believe that all these immigrants have somehow "melted" into a single people. Others say that America is really a mosaic of peoples. A mosaic is small pieces of different colors and shapes that fit together to form a whole picture or pattern.

English immigrants were the first to come to America in large numbers. They set the language and laws of the colonies and, later, the new nation. Then, as America grew into a giant of industry, it welcomed workers from other lands. They did not arrive in a slow, steady stream. Instead, they came in great, flowing, tidal waves. Famine sent waves of Irish, political fighting sent waves of Prussians, and unfair punishment sent waves of Jews. Waves of Swedes, Poles, Chinese, and many others also arrived over the years.

Italians, too, came to America. At first, until about 1880, they were few and mostly from the north. Many were skilled workers or well-to-do people looking for better lives.

But after 1880, most of the newcomers were southern Italians. In ever larger numbers, they left their homeland and crossed the sea in ships. More than 285,000 reached America in 1907 alone! This mighty tide kept up for thirty years until World War I. By that time 4 million Italians had begun new lives as Americans.

Who were these people, and why had they left Italy? Most of them were *contadini*, peasant farmers. They were hardworking, thrifty people whose ancestors had lived off the soil for centuries. Now, however, they could no longer survive on the land.

One reason for their hardships was the system called sharecropping. Little by little, rich men had gained control of the peasants' farms. Most families now worked on land that really belonged to others. For their labor, they were allowed to keep part of the crop. But the share claimed by the owner was unfairly high, and high taxes took another share. The small part left was too little to live on. To keep farming, the farmers had to borrow money from the landowners. At last, after years of being cheated, they were deep in debt. The harder they worked, the more they owed. They were no better off than slaves.

To add to the peasants' troubles, natural disasters struck southern Italy. A disease attacked the grapevines, ruining the wine industry. Then some severe earthquakes hit. One, in 1908, killed two hundred thousand people in Calabria and Sicily. The entire city of Messina was wrecked. The quake caused the sea to draw back, baring the bones of old shipwrecks. Suddenly a huge tidal wave flooded the land.

By then people had been leaving southern Italy for years. Most had held high hopes for the new Italian nation, but they could no longer raise families in such awful poverty. The offer of good jobs and land in America was too strong to resist.

To America they came, in great boatloads. Steamship companies were so eager to carry them that they sent men all through southern Italy to sign up passengers. The cheapest fare, called steerage, cost about thirty-five dollars. Today that doesn't seem to be much money. Most peasants, though, had to sell all they owned to raise it.

Even then, the men could not afford to bring their whole families. Often the husband went to America first. He got a job right away because workers were badly needed. He lived cheaply, saving every penny. Then, one by one, he brought over his children, wife, brothers, and cousins. Before long half his village was living on a street in New York City.

The trip across the ocean was not pleasant. During the journey, which lasted from ten to fifteen days, steerage passengers were jammed together below decks. Some of the largest ships carried two thousand of them at once. Their berths were of iron, with straw mattresses and light blankets. Hundreds of people would share only two washrooms. Everything was dirty, and the noisy engines below made it hard to sleep. Only on deck was there fresh air to breathe.

No wonder everyone rushed above decks when at last America came in sight. There it was, the Statue of Liberty! And there were the towering skyscrapers of New York City, twenty and thirty stories tall! Most Italian peasants had rarely seen buildings as high as four stories. Sometimes they would break into wild cheers. At other times they would fall deeply silent.

On landing, the Italians were taken to an immigrant station. For a number of years they went to a station called Castle Garden, and later, starting in 1892, to Ellis Island. In a huge brick building there, they were given medical checkups. Those with certain illnesses were not allowed to enter the United States. Trachoma, an eye disease, sent some back home. If just one child in a family had this illness, the whole family would have to return to Italy. At least the steamship companies paid the return fare.

Few Italians, though, were sent back. Most went quickly to work. Men did hard labor—digging, hauling, and building—for an average wage of about ten dollars per week. Many women worked in factories.

Immigrants crowd the deck of a ship as it comes into the New York harbor in 1906. One of their first sights was the Statue of Liberty.

Immigrant families spent long hours doing "piecework" for very low wages. This 1889 photo shows a family working in a "sweatshop" in New York City.

Others did "piecework" at home, which meant that they sewed collars or sleeves on clothes at so many cents per piece. Children often helped out with piecework. A family could earn its groceries by sewing far into the night.

Italians worked hard and saved. Many had the idea that they were going back to Italy in a few years. With their savings, they believed, they could buy land there and start again. But not many ever did. They did send money back, though, to help their relatives in the old country.

Life was not easy for the Italians who stayed in America. In the past, most newcomers were welcome. Many of them were fair-skinned people from northern Europe who had some money and skills. But Italians were part of a wave of poor, unskilled people from southern Europe. These darker, "stranger" people were feared by some Americans. The new labor unions worried that Italians would take over their jobs. The union members were partly right, because the newcomers worked very hard for low wages.

Since some Americans feared the "strange" Italians, at times they treated them badly. Italians, in turn, learned to mistrust outsiders. They lived among their own kind in "Little Italys." These were like Italian towns tucked inside American cities. People spoke Italian and kept up the old customs.

In a way, the Little Italys slowed the mixing of Italians into American life. But the mixing happened anyway, mostly through the immigrants' children. All children went to school, either public or Catholic.

They learned to speak and write English, and most important, they learned to think of themselves as Americans. When they grew up, they took jobs in every field. They became doctors, teachers, bankers, and business people. To these Italian Americans, Italy was the foreign land.

Many children of immigrants became famous Americans. Fiorello LaGuardia was New York City's best-known mayor. He was called "The Little Flower," for that's what Fiorello means in English. As a mayor, he was tough, smart, and respected. Above all, he was a reformer who worked for the people.

In sports many Italian Americans have become superstars. Joe DiMaggio was the fleet-footed New York Yankees outfielder. For his speed and grace, he won the nickname "The Yankee Clipper." He is often called the greatest center fielder of all time.

DiMaggio's parents were Italian immigrants living in Martinez, California. His father, who had nine children, ran a crab boat. Since Joe liked catching balls better than catching crabs, he chose baseball for a career. Joe was a batting star as well as a great fielder. His greatest feat was his fifty-six-game hitting streak in 1941, a major league record that still stands today.

Another Italian American became one of the best

heavyweight boxers in ring history. Rocky (Rocco) Marciano was one of six children of an immigrant shoemaker in Brockton, Massachusetts. Rocky was a hard trainer and a harder puncher. Boxing fans admired his courage and the way he could take punishment. Only twice in his career was he knocked off his feet. Though he was one of the smallest heavyweight champions, he won all forty-nine of his fights, forty-three by knockouts.

Size never stops a true champion. Among horse racing fans, little Eddie Arcaro is often called America's greatest jockey. He was born in Cincinnati, Ohio, the son of an immigrant cabdriver. After starting as an exercise boy, he became a jockey. In his thirty years of racing, he won 4,779 races. No one has ever come close to his record of 17 wins in Triple Crown events.

In show business, too, Italian Americans have had great success. Frank Sinatra is one of America's most popular singers, and he has starred in many movies. Liza Minnelli has also become a famous singer and actress. Al Pacino, Robert DeNiro, and Sylvester Stallone are respected actors. Francis Ford Coppola has made a mark as a filmmaker. *The Godfather* and *Apocalypse, Now* are two of his best-known movies.

Some Italian immigrants became well known

Americans in their own right. One is Mother Frances Cabrini, the first American citizen to become a saint of the Roman Catholic church. She was born in the town of Santangelo, in northern Italy. Mother Cabrini came to America in 1889 to help the poor Italian peasants who were coming in such numbers. She started schools, hospitals, and charities that aided many thousands of newly arrived immigrants. In 1946, nearly thirty years after her death, she was named the "Heavenly Patroness of All Emigrants."

Other well-known Italian immigrants came to America more recently. During the 1930s, Benito Mussolini ruled Italy with soldiers and secret police. In a great "brain drain," many scientists and artists fled from his power and settled in other countries, including the United States.

Enrico Fermi was one of these Italian scientists. His work in America helped uncover the secret of the atom. Fermi won the Nobel Prize, a scientist's highest honor. Two other immigrant scientists, Emilio Segrè and Salvador Luria, also won Nobel Prizes.

Arturo Toscanini, a famous music conductor, arrived in America at about the same time. Toscanini was soon asked to conduct a leading radio orchestra. Week after week for seventeen years, he directed fine music to America's ears.

Salvemini, the historian, Tucci and Ascoli, the

writers, Fano and Rasetti, the scientists—all these
Italians gave their gifts to their new country. In fact,
the flow of Italians to America has never really
stopped. About twenty-five thousand still arrive each
year. They no longer travel in steerage or pass
through Ellis Island. But like all immigrants, they
bring their dreams for a better life.

These newcomers join about 9 million other Italian Americans. Since most did not settle far from
where they landed in New York City, seven out of ten
live in the Northeast today. Many more did move on
to Chicago, Los Angeles, and San Francisco. Large
groups have also settled in rural America.

Over the years the Little Italys have slowly
shrunk away. The days of the "great wave" are over
now. Still, many Italian Americans go back to visit
the old neighborhoods. They like the feeling of the
open markets, the cafés, and the sidewalk card games.

A few times a year, the old gaiety comes alive in
full force. The feast of Our Lady Of Mount Carmel
draws crowds to East Harlem in New York City.
Saint Gennaro's feast is marked with a two-day street
fair in Greenwich Village. The fun reaches its peak
after dark when lights, music, and the smell of hot
food fill the air. People can barely move through the
crowded streets.

Most of the visitors to these celebrations, however, are young people who speak no Italian. They know little of their grandparents' struggles in Italy. People of German, Irish, Jewish, and Spanish backgrounds mix freely with them.

In one sense, there is little difference among all these smiling faces. These people have become, simply, Americans.

But in another sense, they are still partly German, Irish, and Italian. One day they will want to know more about their heritage in faraway lands—and rightly so. For it is the blend of all their rich ways of life that has made America great.

Appendix

Italian Consulates in the United States and Canada

The Italian consulates in the United States and Canada want to help Americans and Canadians understand Italian ways. For information and resource materials about Italy, contact the consulate or embassy nearest you.

U.S. Consulates

Boston, Massachusetts
Consulate General of Italy
101 Tremont Street
Boston, Massachusetts 02108
Phone (617) 542-0483

Chicago, Illinois
Consulate General of Italy
625 N. Michigan Avenue
Chicago, Illinois 60611
Phone (312) 943-0703

Detroit, Michigan
Consulate of Italy
1900 The Executive Plaza Building
1200 Sixth Avenue
Detroit, Michigan 48226
Phone (313) 963-8460

New Orleans, Louisiana
Consulate General of Italy
708 Cotton Exchange Building
231 Carondolet Street
New Orleans, Louisiana 70130
Phone (504) 524-2271

New York, New York
Consulate General of Italy
690 Park Avenue
New York, New York 10021
Phone (212) 737-9100
Philadelphia, Pennsylvania
Consulate General of Italy
2128 Locust Street
Philadelphia, Pennsylvania 19103
Phone (215) 732-7436
San Francisco, California
Consulate General of Italy
2590 Webster Street
San Francisco, California 94115
Phone (415) 931-4924

Canadian Consulates

Montreal, Quebec
Consulate General of Italy
3489 Drummond Avenue
Montreal, Quebec H3G 1X6
Phone 849-8351
Ottawa, Ontario
Embassy of Italy
275 Slater Street 11th Floor
Ottawa, Ontario K1P 5H9
Phone (613) 232-2401
Vancouver, British Columbia
Consulate General of Italy
1200 Burrard Street
Suite 505
Vancouver, British Columbia V6Z 2C7
Phone 685-8451

Glossary

agnolotti—macaroni shaped like "little fat lambs"

al dente—pasta that is boiled not too soft but "firm to the tooth"

antipasto—an appetizer dish of cheese slices, cold cuts, and vegetables

bacalà—a dish made with dried salt codfish

(la) Befana—the good witch who brings gifts on January 6, Epiphany

bocce—a game in which the players roll wooden balls on a long, narrow cinder court

briscola—a popular card game

brodetto—a rich fish soup

bucatini—macaroni shaped like little holes

caffe lungo—coffee thinned with water

caffelatte—"coffee-milk"; an even mixture of coffee and hot milk

calcio—soccer

cannelloni—large macaroni tubes stuffed with ricotta cheese and chopped meat

cannoli—cheese-filled pastries

capitone—a special eel dish eaten on Christmas Eve in the area of Rome

cappelletti—little dough "hats" stuffed with meat

cappucino—coffee lightened with a little milk

Carnevale—"farewell to meat"; the season of feasting and fun just before Lent

catenaccio—a style of defense used by Italy's World Cup soccer team in 1970

contadini—peasant farmers

culatelli—a very tasty, spicy ham

cullurelli—deep-fried Christmas pastries sprinkled with powdered sugar

(il) Duce—the "Leader"; the name given to the dictator Mussolini

(l') Epifania—the feast of Epiphany, or Little Christmas, on January 6

espresso—a type of strong, black coffee

farfalle—macaroni shaped like butterflies

Festa del Grillo—the cricket festival held each spring in Florence

fettucine—ribbon-shaped noodles

galleria—a covered shopping mall

gelato—ice cream

gnocchi—boiled pellets of mashed potato and flour

gondola—a special boat used on the canals of Venice, poled along by a boatman

lasagna—a baked dish of broad noodles, sauce, meatballs, and cheese

libretto—"little book"; a nickname for pizza slices folded in half

liceo—a high school

(il) Lotto—a national lottery based on the game of lotto

maestro—"master"; the name children call their teachers

Mamma mia!—"My mother!"; a phrase often used to show excitement or wonder

Mangia!—"Eat!"

manicotti—long, flat macaroni shells filled with soft cheese

Martedi Grasso—Shrove Tuesday, the day before Ash Wednesday.

minestrone—a thick vegetable soup

morra—a finger-counting game

mostaccioli—chocolate honey cookies shaped like saints or animals

mozzarella—a cheese used in making many common dishes

nonna—grandmother

pallino—a small wooden ball used in the game of bocce

panettone—a special Christmas currant cake

panforte—nut-filled gingerbread, served on Christmas Eve

(Il) Papa—the Pope

pasta—dough made from durum wheat; this name is also used for all the macaroni and spaghetti shapes made from it

pazienza—"patience"

piazza—a town square, often in front of a church

pitte—colored breads popular in Calabria

polenta—a puddinglike dish made from ground corn

presepio—a model of the Bethlehem scene

Prima il dovere, poi il piacere—a saying meaning, "Duty first, then pleasure"

ravioli—dough pockets filled with spinach, cheese, or chopped meat

Risorgimento—"Rising again"; the movement to win Italy's national freedom in the 1850s

scopone—a popular card game

Scoppio del Carro—"Explosion of the Car"; a festival held in Florence on the day before Easter

scuola elementare—"elementary school"

scuola media—"middle school"; similar to an American junior high school

sirocco—a hot wind that blows from the Sahara Desert across the Mediterranean Sea to Italy.

spumoni—rich ice cream

tarantella—a lively group folk dance

torrone—nougat candy

tortellini—macaroni shaped like little twists

Unni rinna, unni farina—a saying meaning, "In some places sand, in some places flour"

ziti—tube-shaped macaroni, sometimes baked with sauce and cheese

Selected Bibliography

Calvino, Italo. *Italian Folktales*, selected and retold by Italo Calvino, translated by George Martin. New York: Harcourt, Brace, Jovanovich, 1980.

Davidson, Spencer. "Italy: Land of Woe and Wonder." *Time*. December 21, 1981, 50-53.

Gambino, Richard. *Blood of my Blood: The Dilemma of the Italian Americans*. New York: Doubleday, 1975.

Gambino, Richard. *Bread and Roses*. New York: Seaview Press, 1981.

Gendel, Milton, ed. *An Illustrated History of Italy*. New York: McGraw-Hill, 1966.

Iorizzo, Luciano J., and Mondello, Salvatore. *The Italian-Americans*. Boston: Twayne Publishers, 1971.

Levi, Carlo, and Reismann, Janos. *Eternal Italy*. New York: The Viking Press, 1960.

Salvadori, Massimo. *Italy*. Englewood Cliffs, N.J.: Prentice-Hall, 1965.

Spicer, Dorothy Gladys. *Festivals of Western Europe*. New York: H.W. Wilson, 1958.

Tifft, Wilton; Dunne, Thomas; and Macek, Mila. *Ellis Island*. New York: W.W. Norton, 1971.

Winwar, Frances. *The Land and People of Italy*. New York: J.B. Lippincott, 1972.

Index

About the Author

Anthony Mario DiFranco's short stories and articles have appeared in a variety of publications, and his short story, "The Brave," won the Catholic Press Association's first prize for fiction in 1981. *Italy: Balanced on the Edge of Time* is his first book for young people. The author credits his large extended family for providing him with abun-  dant material for writing; just the aunts, uncles, first cousins, nieces, and nephews in this prolific clan number 105.

Born in New York City, Mr. DiFranco studied at Fordham University, where he received the B.A. in classical languages and the M.A. in English, and at St. John's University, where he earned the professional diploma in school administration. Since 1974, the author has taught writing, literature, and journalism in the English department of Suffolk County Community College. He lives in Northport, New York, with his wife Adrienne and their four children.